The World of Food

First Steck-Vaughn Edition 1992

This edition first published in 1987 by Raintree Publishers Inc.,
a Division of Steck-Vaughn Company.

Text copyright © 1987 by Raintree Publishers Inc., translated
by Alison Taurel.
© 1981 Hachette

All rights reserved. No part of the material protected by this copyright
may be reproduced or utilized in any form by any means, electronic or
mechanical, including photocopying, recording, or by any information
storage and retrieval system, without permission in writing from
Steck-Vaughn Company, P.O. Box 26015, Austin, TX 78755.
Printed in the United States of America.

Library of Congress Number: 86-31631

2 3 4 5 6 7 8 9   94 93 92

Library of Congress Cataloging in Publication Data

Rocard, Ann.
  Ask about the world of food.

  Translation of: La cuisine des petits.
  Summary: Answers questions commonly asked
about food, such as its preparation, health, nutrition,
and food customs of other countries.
  1. Food—Juvenile literature. 2. Cookery—
Juvenile literature. [1. Food. 2. Food habits]
I. Title.
TX355.R6313 1987   641   86-31631
ISBN 0-8172-2885-3 (lib. bdg.)
ISBN 0-8172-2897-7 (softcover)

Cover illustration: David Schweitzer

Ask About
The World of Food

Austin, Texas

Contents

Table of measurements 7

Food for health and happiness

Does soup make you grow? 8
Why shouldn't you swallow things whole? 8
Why can't I eat whenever I want to? 10
Why can't I just eat what I want? 10
Why do I have to wash my hands before eating? 10
Why do I have to eat before school? 12
Why do people eat cheese? 12
Do babies eat the same food as grown-ups? 12
Why can't I use a lot of salt? 14
Is there such a thing as blue candy? 14
What happens if I eat too much? 14
Why can't children drink alcohol? 16
Why are there different kinds of milk? 16
What would happen if I didn't drink a thing? 16
What would happen if I swallowed a pit or a seed? 18
Why does some food need to be kept in the refrigerator? 18
Does some fruit cause stomachaches? 18
Why is there white bread and dark bread? 20
Why can't I just eat candy? 20
Do people eat the same things all over the world? 20

Fruit and vegetables 22
Calories 24
Vitamins 26
Protein, carbohydrates, and fats 28

Food around the world

Breakfast, what a treat! 30
Muesli 31

Salted cake 32
Coconut candy 33
Steak tartare 34
Cheesecake 35
Garden salad 36
Apple cake 37
Tabouleh salad 38
Cinnamon oranges 39
Pineapple or avocado delight 40
Popcorn 41
Cucumber in yogurt 42
Almond rice 43
Picnic 44
When the weather's nice! 45
Raw fish 46
Fruit salad 47
Lemon mushrooms 48
Banana cake 49
Tomatoes with shrimp 50
Sweet rounds 51
Chicken in papillotes 52
Mocha cream 53
Grilled ham and cheese sandwiches 54
Bread pudding 55
Pizza 56
Ice cream 57
Ham surprise 58
Charlotte 59
Buffet 60
Happy partying! 61

Glossary 62
Index 63

Table of Measurements

1 cup = 8 ounces | 1 tablespoon = 3 teaspoons | 1 pound = 16 ounces

1 cup = 1/2 pint | 1 teaspoon = 1/3 tablespoon | 1 pint = 1 pound

1 gallon = 4 quarts | 1 quart = 2 pints | 1 pint = 2 cups

Butter: one-pound package

Cut in four pieces, each piece equals 1/4 pound or 1/2 cup. | Cut in two pieces, each piece equals 1/2 pound or 1 cup. | The whole package equals one pound or two cups.

Milk or other liquid:

1 cup = 1/2 pint | 1/2 cup = 4 ounces | 1/2 gallon = 64 ounces

Signs:

Oven must be lit. | Can be made alone. | You'll need help.

Food for health and happiness

Does soup make you grow?

Yes, but it is not the only thing that does. All good food nourishes, builds, and repairs your body. It also makes your hair and nails grow and helps mend broken bones. Food provides you with energy. Just like cars need quality gasoline to run well, your body needs quality food.

Why shouldn't you swallow things whole?

It is very important to chew your food well. When you chew, your teeth crush the food. It then gets mixed with saliva and is liquified so that your stomach will not have to overwork at breaking down the food. If you swallow something whole, your stomach has to work very hard which causes you to get a stomachache. Also, you run the risk of choking when you swallow things whole.

Why can't I eat whenever I want to?

Eating snacks all day long is not good for you. Your stomach needs to rest in between meals. Snacking also increases your chances of getting cavities which are small holes in your teeth. You should eat three healthy meals a day—breakfast, lunch, and dinner—and brush your teeth after every meal.

Why can't I just eat what I want?

Your body needs certain things in order for you to be healthy. Each day you should eat fruit, vegetables, grains, dairy products, and protein such as meat, fish, chicken, or an egg.

Why do I have to wash my hands before eating?

Your hands constantly get dirty and become covered with germs each day. Because you use your hands to eat, it is important to wash them with soap and water before coming to the table. This may prevent some germs from entering your body. For the same reason, you should carefully wash the dishes and the table, too. Most fruits and vegetables also need to be washed before eating because they often contain dirt and chemicals.

Why do I have to eat before school?

If you don't eat until lunchtime, you will be tired, dizzy, and unable to concentrate on your work. Breakfast gives you the energy that you need to enjoy your work and play.

Why do people eat cheese?

Cheese, milk, and certain vegetables such as spinach, cauliflower, and broccoli contain an important element called calcium. Calcium strengthens bones and teeth. It is one of the many minerals necessary for good health. For example, iron is essential for healthy blood. It is found in fruit, vegetables, grains, meat, and nuts.

Do babies eat the same food as grown-ups?

No. At first, babies drink milk and fruit juice. Later, they begin to eat mashed vegetables and stewed fruit. After a baby's teeth grow, he or she can start to chew solid food. The bigger a child becomes, the more adult types of food the youngster can eat. All adults don't eat the same types of food either. A construction worker and a secretary require quite different meals.

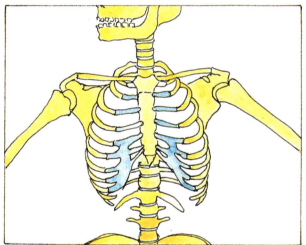

Why can't I use a lot of salt?

A dash of salt can improve the flavor of food, but too much salt can ruin the flavor completely. Salt is also very unhealthy. Instead of salting your food, try using other seasonings such as parsley, fennel, mint, chives, thyme, cinnamon, or rosemary.

Is there such a thing as blue candy?

Blue candy that you might sometimes eat contains harmful chemicals that create its blue color. There is no food that is naturally blue. It is important to read labels on packaged foods to avoid harmful substances.

What happens if I eat too much?

If you eat an entire cake or box of chocolates, you will get sick. If you overeat at every meal, you will probably get fat because your body does not need so much food.

Why can't children drink alcohol?

Alcohol that is found in beer, wine, and liquor is very powerful. It destroys cells in all parts of the body especially the brain and liver. People who drink a lot of alcohol become very ill. Beverages such as tea, coffee, and some kinds of soda pop contain caffeine which is a stimulant. It can make you nervous and unable to sleep.

Why are there different kinds of milk?

You can buy cows' milk in various forms depending upon your personal taste. There is "whole" milk which has none of its butterfat removed. Milk that is labeled "2%" or "1%" has had its butterfat partially removed. Milk that has had all the butterfat removed is called "skim" milk. You can also buy milk in powdered or condensed forms.

What would happen if I didn't drink a thing?

Not only would you be very thirsty, you would become very ill. There is water in each cell of your body that needs to be replaced every day. Drinking eight glasses of water each day is recommended. It is better to drink water in between meals than with meals. Fruit and vegetable juices are also very good for you, and they are delicious.

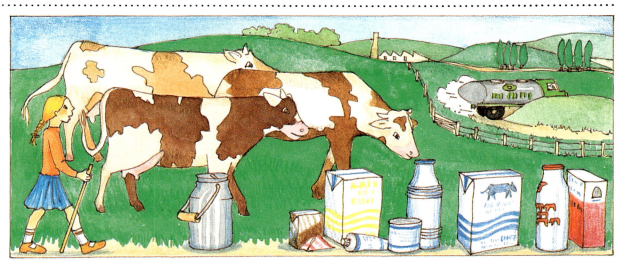

What would happen if I swallowed a pit or a seed?

A fruit pit or seed is like a pebble. It cannot be digested by humans. But don't worry, the pit will pass through your system, and a tree will not grow from your stomach. Sometimes, however, a pit or seed may get stuck in your throat, stomach, or intestine and cause discomfort and problems.

Why does some food need to be kept in the refrigerator?

Keeping food cold lengthens the time before the food spoils. Food keeps even longer in the freezer.

Does some fruit cause stomachaches?

Fruit that is overripe or not ripe enough can cause stomachaches. Cherries, strawberries, oranges, and peaches can also cause stomachaches if you eat too many of them at once. Some foods can be dangerous to eat. You should never eat berries and mushrooms that grow wild. These may be poisonous and could kill you.

cherry or mirabel plum • apricot and plum
peach and nectarine • avocado and mango

briony • foxglove • nightshade • fuchsia
phalloid Amanita • spring Amanita • fly Amanita • panther Amanita

Why is there white bread and dark bread?

Bread is made with flour. Flour is made from ground wheat or other grains. Each grain of wheat is enclosed by a small brown skin. If the skin is left on the grain, the flour and bread will be dark. If the skin is removed, the flour and bread will be white. It is healthier to eat breads and rice with the skin left on the grain.

Why can't I just eat candy?

When you eat a lot of candy, you are eating too much sugar. Sugar doesn't contain the vitamins and minerals necessary for good health. Also, sugar causes cavities and you will have to go to the dentist to get the cavities filled. It is a good idea to avoid sugar. You need to brush your teeth after eating candy.

Do people eat the same things all over the world?

No. People usually eat what is available in their location, and plants and animals are different in various parts of the world. Africans eat more coconut than Americans. People that live near the ocean eat more seafood than those living in the desert. The people of a certain country or region have certain eating customs, too. In America, many people are fond of ice cream, hot dogs, pizza, or salads. The Japanese eat a lot of rice, seaweed, and raw fish.

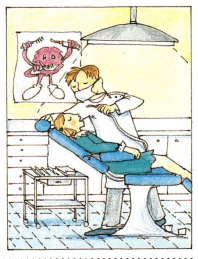

Fruit and vegetables

People usually eat different fruit and vegetables according to the season. Usually you find cherries in June and grapes in September and October.

In season in the spring: artichokes, lettuce, spinach. **At the end of spring:** strawberries, cherries, raspberries, rhubarb.

In season in the summer: squash, eggplant, tomatoes, peppers, green beans, melons, peaches, apricots, prunes.

The weather is also an important factor in determining the food that people eat. Many people like to eat soup when it is cold or wet outside. Ice cream is very popular when the weather is warm.

In season in the fall: mushrooms, pumpkins, grapes, apples, pears, various nuts, corn.

In season in the winter: cabbage, brussels sprouts, cauliflower, leeks, oranges, tangerines, apples, kiwifruit.

Calories

Food gives energy to the body to keep you alive, growing, and active. This energy comes from calories found in food. Not everyone needs the same amount of calories each day.

Some foods contain a lot of calories; others have just a few. For example, if you eat one candy bar, you will have eaten as many calories as you would find in nine carrots or four apples.

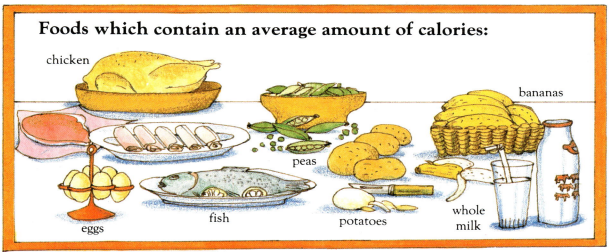

Vitamins

Vitamins are substances in food that are important in maintaining good health. Long ago, sailors who went on long journeys came down with a disease called scurvy. Scurvy is caused by a lack of vitamin C which is found in fruit and leafy vegetables. In the following pictures, you will see that each of the many vitamins is useful to a certain part of your body or in certain activities such as growth and eyesight.

VITAMIN A
For growth, eyesight, skin, and circulation.

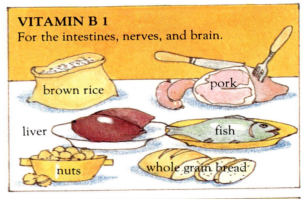

VITAMIN B 1
For the intestines, nerves, and brain.

VITAMIN B 2
For growth, respiration and the skin.

VITAMIN B 5
For the skin, hair, and nails.

VITAMIN B 6
For the blood and the processing of fats.

VITAMINS B and C
For growth, to fight fatigue, and for the blood.

VITAMIN B 12
For growth, to fight fatigue, for the blood, skin and brain.

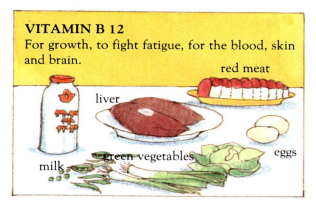

VITAMIN C
For resistance to illness, to build a healthy body, bones, and muscles.

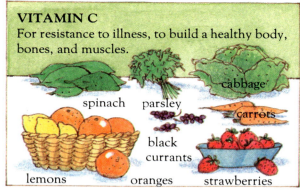

VITAMIN E
For the muscles and brain.

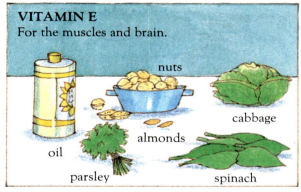

VITAMIN D
For strong bones and teeth.

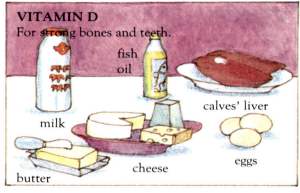

BIOTIN
For building a healthy body, bones, and brain, and for the blood and hair.

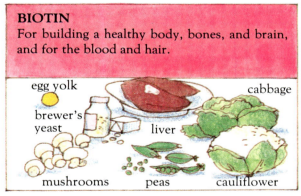

VITAMIN K
For growth and for the clotting of blood.

NIACIN
For growth, the nerves and brain, and the skin.

FOLIC ACID
For production of hemoglobin in red blood cells.

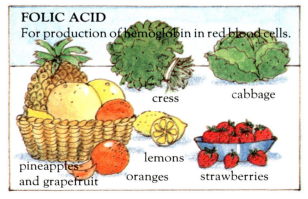

Protein, carbohydrates, and fats

Protein, carbohydrates, and fats are necessary to maintain good health. The ideal diet is high in carbohydrates and low in fats, with a limited amount of protein.

CARBOHYDRATES

They bring warmth, energy, and strength to the body. They supply vital nutrients and fiber.

They are mainly found in:

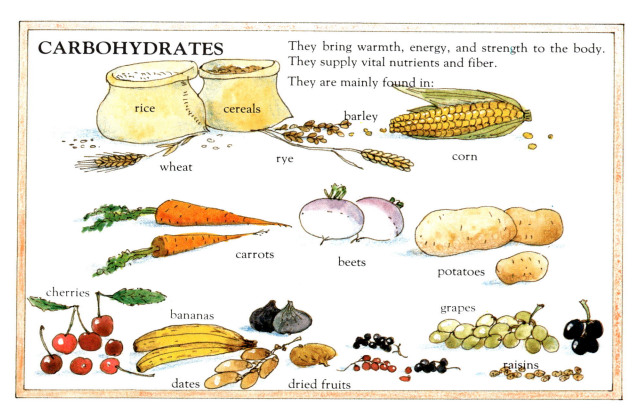

FATS

They give the body energy, protect against heat and cold, and cushion vital organs.

They are mainly found in:

Breakfast, what a treat!

corn flakes
1 cup orange juice
1 carton yogurt
1 cup milk
honey or jelly
butter
whole grain bread or rolls
1 piece cheese
1 hard boiled egg
dried fruit
sugar
apple

Mix one cup milk, a little sugar, and corn flakes.

Prepare one cup orange juice — one carton yogurt

whole grain bread — or rolls — butter — jelly — or honey

dried apricots — raisins — dried bananas

crunchy apple

If it is going to be a tiring day, you may also eat:

boiled egg — one piece of cheese

30

Salted cake

2 cups flour
4 eggs
1/4 cup oil
1 large piece ham
1 cup milk
1/2 cup Swiss cheese
1 packet yeast

Mix in a large bowl:

two cups flour   one packet yeast   1/4 cup oil   one cup milk

Cut a large piece of ham (or bacon)
into small pieces.
Grate the cheese.

small pieces of ham

grated Swiss cheese

Add to mixture.
Prepare a baking pan.
Rub the inside with oil,
and pour in the mixture.

oil

Have an adult put the pan in the oven. Bake at 350° for one hour.

You can eat the cake hot or cold.

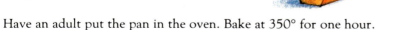

Coconut candy

1 egg
1 cup powdered sugar
2 cups grated coconut
1/4 teaspoon salt
1 teaspoon vanilla

Mix in a large bowl: one cup powdered sugar, one egg, 1/4 tsp. salt, 1 tsp. vanilla, two cups grated coconut

Place a piece of tin foil on a cookie sheet.

Using a teaspoon, make little patties and put them on the foil.

An adult may place the cookie sheet in the oven. Bake at 400° for twenty minutes.

Eastern Countries	# Steak tartare

2 eggs
1 tablespoon oil
2 teaspoons mayonnaise
1/2 teaspoon salt
mustard
chives
capers
pickles
pepper
parsley
chopped onion
1 pound ground beef

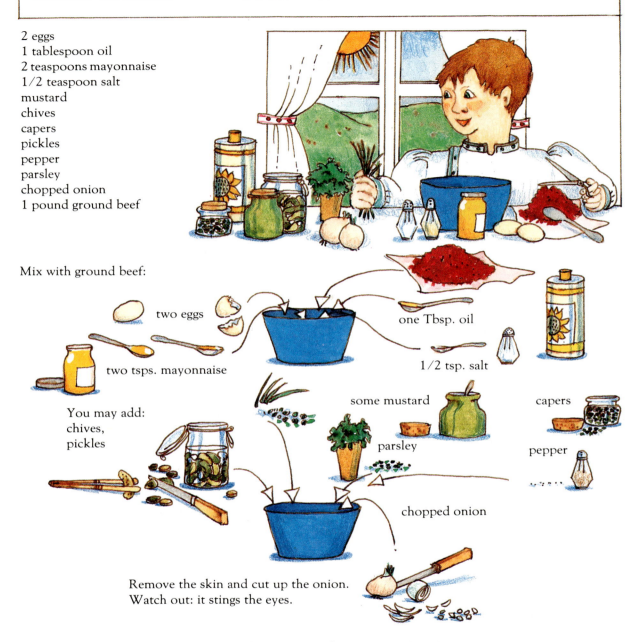

Mix with ground beef:

two eggs

two tsps. mayonnaise

one Tbsp. oil

1/2 tsp. salt

some mustard

capers

parsley

pepper

You may add:
chives,
pickles

chopped onion

Remove the skin and cut up the onion.
Watch out: it stings the eyes.

Mix well and place the bowl in the refrigerator until ready to serve.

Cheesecake

CRUST:
1/2 cup butter
1/2 cup sugar
2 eggs
2 cups flour
1 tablespoon baking powder
1/4 teaspoon salt

CHEESECAKE:
2 eggs
1 - 12 ounce package
   cream cheese
3/4 cup sugar
1 teaspoon vanilla
1 tablespoon flour

Use pre-made piecrust
or make a piecrust with the help of an adult. Mix in a bowl:

two cups flour
two eggs
1/2 cup butter
1/2 cup sugar
1/4 tsp. salt
and one Tbsp. baking powder

Put the dough on a clean table and get a rolling pin.
Roll out the dough and place it in a pie tin.

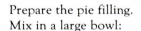

Prepare the pie filling.
Mix in a large bowl:

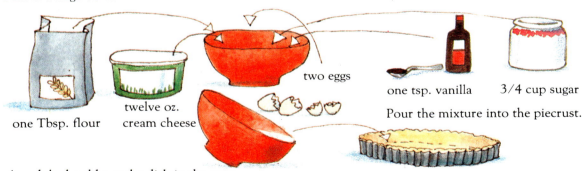

one Tbsp. flour
twelve oz. cream cheese
two eggs
one tsp. vanilla
3/4 cup sugar

Pour the mixture into the piecrust.

An adult should put the dish in the oven.
Bake at 425° for one-half hour.
Cool before serving.

35

Garden salad

lettuce
nuts
small pieces of cheese
1/2 teaspoon salt or herbs
raisins
garlic
1 tablespoon vinegar
3 tablespoons oil
croutons

head lettuce   romaine lettuce   leaf lettuce

Wash the lettuce in cold water. Dry and tear the lettuce into small pieces.

Put the pieces into a salad bowl and add:

nuts

croutons

cheese

1/2 tsp. salt or herbs

You may add some raisins or

small pieces of garlic

raisins

Prepare the dressing:

three Tbsp. oil   one Tbsp. vinegar

Pour over the salad.
Mix well just before serving.

France

Apple cake

1 carton plain yogurt
3 cups powdered sugar
3 cups flour
1/2 cup oil
1 packet yeast
4 eggs
4 apples

Mix in a large bowl:

one carton plain yogurt

one packet yeast

three cups flour

three cups powdered sugar

Add four eggs

1/2 cup oil

Peel four apples and remove the cores.

Then cut the apples into pieces.

Prepare a baking dish. Wipe the inside with oil.

oil

Pour in the mixture.

An adult should place the baking dish in the oven. Bake at 400° for one-half hour. Cool before serving.

| Middle East | **Tabouleh salad** | |

1 cup bulgur wheat
1 large tomato
juice of three lemons
2 tablespoons oil
1/2 teaspoon salt
parsley
fresh mint

Squeeze the juice from three lemons and chop the tomato into pieces.

Pour the bulgur into a bowl and add:

the juice of three lemons   1/2 tsp. salt   one tomato   two Tbsp. oil

Cut and add the parsley and fresh mint leaves and mix well.
Put salad bowl in refrigerator until you are ready to serve.

Cinnamon oranges

North Africa

four oranges
raisins
one tablespoon powdered sugar
one teaspoon cinnamon

Peel four oranges and divide into segments.

Place the segments on a plate in a flower shape.

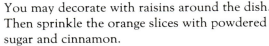

You may decorate with raisins around the dish. Then sprinkle the orange slices with powdered sugar and cinnamon.

 one tsp. cinnamon    one Tbsp. powdered sugar

Place the dish in the refrigerator for several hours and serve chilled.

Pineapple or avocado delight

U.S.A.

pineapple or avocados
walnuts
1 can crab meat
salt or herbs
celery
cooked corn
2 tablespoons fresh cream
4 tablespoons mayonnaise
lettuce leaves
raisins

Prepare the pineapple or avocados.

Cut off the top of the pineapple and hollow it out with a knife.

Cut the avocados in two and remove the pits.

chunks of pineapple

Mix in a salad bowl:
pieces of walnut

a can of crab meat

cooked kernel corn

If you want, add some celery, cut into pieces.

To make the sauce, add:

two Tbsp. fresh cream

four Tbsp. mayonnaise

salt or herbs

Mix well and fill the pineapple (or the avocados). Place them on a platter decorated with lettuce leaves and raisins.

U.S.A. # Popcorn

This is easy to make, but an adult needs to watch the stove with you.
Pour into a large saucepan:

one Tbsp. oil

Warm the saucepan at low heat.
Pour into the saucepan:

three Tbsp. popcorn kernels

Cover with a lid, and move the saucepan back and forth over the heat. POP! The kernels will explode one after another.

Turn the heat off after five minutes, and pour the popped kernels into a large bowl.

Pour two Tbsp. butter on top and mix well.
You may also top the popcorn with cheese or something sweet.

| Bulgaria | # Cucumber in yogurt | |

1 cucumber
1/2 teaspoon salt
1/4 teaspoon pepper
chives or tarragon
parsley
1/4 minced garlic
2 cartons plain yogurt

Pour the two plain yogurts into a large bowl.

Beat with a fork.

Peel a large cucumber and cut it into small pieces.

some chives

or tarragon

parsley

cucumber

1/2 tsp. salt and, if you like, 1/4 tsp. pepper

and, if you like, 1/4 tsp. minced garlic.

Chill in the refrigerator before serving.

Almond rice

Norway

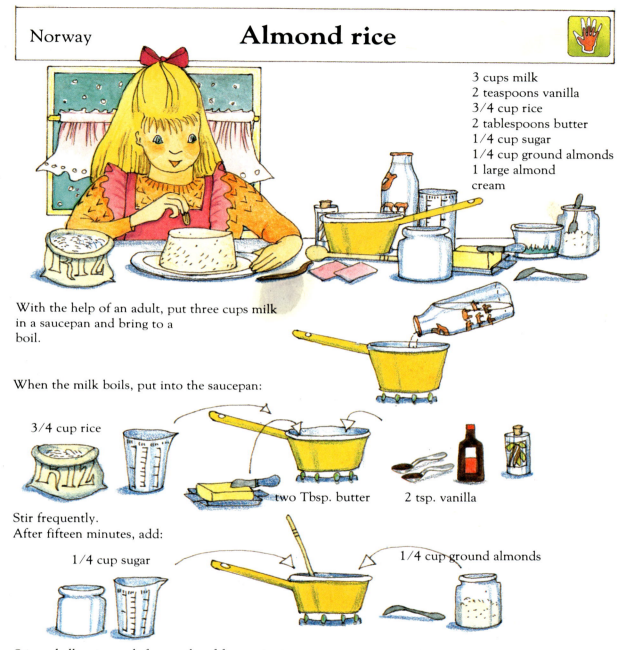

3 cups milk
2 teaspoons vanilla
3/4 cup rice
2 tablespoons butter
1/4 cup sugar
1/4 cup ground almonds
1 large almond
cream

With the help of an adult, put three cups milk in a saucepan and bring to a boil.

When the milk boils, put into the saucepan:

3/4 cup rice   two Tbsp. butter   2 tsp. vanilla

Stir frequently.
After fifteen minutes, add:

1/4 cup sugar   1/4 cup ground almonds

Stir and allow to cook for another fifteen minutes.
Then slide the big almond into the mixture.
This dish may be eaten hot or cold with a little fresh cream.

Who will find the big almond?

Picnic

whole grain bread
ham
cheese
French bread
butter or mayonnaise
tomatoes
olives
cucumbers
pickles
oil
chili pepper
chicken

What do you need
to pack for a picnic?

Some sandwiches
Spread the butter on one side of the bread,
then add the ham
and some cheese.

OR: If you prefer, you may substitute French bread.
Cut up pieces of cooked chicken,
slices of pickles, olives,
cucumbers . . .

tomatoes

Mix all the ingredients together,
and place them into the bread.
Wrap each sandwich in plastic.

one Tbsp. oil

pieces of chili pepper

bread

When the weather's nice!

carrots
hard-boiled eggs
fresh fruit
cheese
water
juice
cake

Bring some cheese along with you and peeled carrots.

plastic wrap

and eggs that you have cooked for ten minutes in a saucepan of boiling water,

washed or easily-peeled fruit

apple   pear
tangerine

And, if you like, a piece of cake.

Don't forget a bottle of water or juice.

Raw fish

fresh, raw seafood
cooked, cold rice
vinegar
radish
ginger

Select some fresh, raw seafood.
For example:

flounder salmon caviar (fish eggs) tuna sardines cuttlefish large shrimp

Wash the fish in cold water, and remove the skin and bones.

Cut the fish into pieces.

Put them on a plate.

Prepare a small bowl of vinegar for dipping the fish.

Add a side dish of cooked, cold rice.

You may add
peeled and grated radish
and ginger (watch out, it's strong).
This is eaten with chopsticks.

Fruit salad

lemon juice
apples
pears
bananas
oranges
cherries
plums
kiwifruit
mangoes
pineapple
orange juice
canned fruit
raisins
prunes
nuts
sugar

You may use all kinds of fruit.

Peel and cut the fruit into pieces

Put it all into a salad bowl and add

juice from canned fruit
fresh-squeezed orange and lemon juice
raisins and pitted prunes
nuts
four Tbsp. sugar

Put the salad bowl in the refrigerator.

Lemon mushrooms

mushrooms
lettuce leaves
radishes
tomatoes
1/2 teaspoon salt or herbs
1 tablespoon oil
juice of 1 lemon
parsley
pickles

Cut off the bottom of the mushrooms.
Wash the mushrooms well and pat dry.

Cut them into slices.

Place a washed and drained lettuce
leaf on each plate. Add some
sliced radish, pieces of tomato,
and the mushroom slices.

To make the sauce, mix the following in a bowl:

the juice of one lemon   1/2 tsp. salt or herbs   1 Tbsp. oil

Pour a little sauce on each plate.
You may decorate with parsley and pickles.

Banana cake

seven bananas
4 teaspoons flour
2 tablespoons butter (melted)
2 eggs
4 tablespoons raisins
4 tablespoons sugar
2 teaspoons cinnamon

Peel seven bananas
Mash them with a fork. Mix the bananas in a bowl with:

two Tbsp. melted butter, which you melt in a small saucepan over low heat with the help of an adult.

Add
two eggs and
four Tbsp. raisins.

Mix well.
Prepare a baking dish.
Rub the inside with oil.
Pour the mixture into the dish and sprinkle:

four Tbsp. sugar
and two tsp. cinnamon on top.

An adult should place the dish in a 450° oven for one-half hour.
This dessert may be eaten cold or hot.

Tomatoes with shrimp

6 tomatoes
1 cup cooked shrimp
parsley
4 tablespoons mayonnaise
lettuce leaves

Wash and drain the tomatoes.
Cut out the top of the tomato and hollow out the inside.

In a salad bowl, mix:
four Tbsp. mayonnaise
the juice from the tomatoes
and one cup cooked shrimp.

Cut some parsley into small pieces and add it to the mixture.

Fill the tomatoes with this mixture and replace the tops.

Put the tomatoes on a dish decorated with lettuce leaves.
Place the dish in the refrigerator until ready to serve.

Sweet rounds

Germany

1 1/4 cups flour
1/2 cup sugar
1 teaspoon vanilla
3/4 cup softened butter
1 egg
jelly or jam

In a salad bowl mix:

1 1/4 cups flour

one teaspoon vanilla

one egg

3/4 cup softened butter

1/2 cup sugar

Take a little dough in your hands and make a ball.

Flatten each little ball between your hands.

balls of dough

Place the flattened balls on greased tin foil placed on a cookie sheet.

oil

An adult should put the cookie sheet in an oven heated to 400°.
When the cakes are light brown, "glue" them one on top of another with jam or jelly.

jam or jelly

Chicken in papillotes

pieces of chicken
tomato slices
thyme
rosemary
mustard

Place pieces of chicken on small sheets of tin foil.
Next to the chicken, place:

thyme and rosemary

and tomato slices.

Spread mustard thinly over the chicken.

papillotes

Wrap the tin foil around the chicken.

An adult should place the wrapped packets in a hot oven.
Bake at 400° for one hour. Each person opens their own "papillote" for eating.

Mocha cream

3 teaspoons instant coffee
4 tablespoons sugar
6 small chocolate pudding cups
walnuts
almonds

Mix: six small chocolate pudding cups from the grocery store, 3 tsp. instant coffee, and four Tbsp. sugar.

Add ground walnuts or almonds.

Decorate with halved walnuts.
Put the dish in the refrigerator.
Mocha cream should be well chilled before serving.

Grilled ham and cheese sandwiches

whole grain bread
butter
ham
cheese

Spread some butter on each slice of bread.

Slice some ham to the size of the bread.

Place a slice of ham on each slice of bread (butter side up). Slice or grate some cheese and place it on the ham.

Place the sandwiches open-faced on a cookie sheet.

Use a timer for counting the minutes.

An adult should put the cookie sheet in an oven heated to 450°. Heat the sandwiches but watch carefully to make sure they don't burn.

| England | **Bread pudding** | |

1 1/8 cups flour
1/2 teaspoon salt
1/2 cup dried bread pieces or crumbs
3/4 cup butter
1 1/2 cups milk
1/2 cup raisins or figs
1/2 cup sugar
a little ground ginger

In a large bowl, mix:

1 1/8 cup flour
1/2 cup dried bread pieces
1/2 tsp. salt

Then you add:

3/4 cup butter
1 1/2 cups milk
1/2 cup sugar
1/2 cup raisins or figs (cut into pieces)
If you want, add a little ground ginger.

Prepare an oven-proof dish. Rub the inside with oil.

Pour the mixture into the dish. Cover the dish with tin foil.

An adult should put the dish into the oven. Bake at 325° for two hours.

Italy

Pizza

pizza crust mix
1/2 cup tomato sauce
1/2 tablespoon oil
mushrooms
grated cheese
sausage, hamburger, or pepperoni
salt, pepper
onions
black olives
anchovies
  (optional)

Follow the directions on the box of pizza crust mix to make the dough.

Roll the dough out
on a greased cookie sheet
with a floured rolling pin.

Spread the
tomato sauce on the dough.

Then add:

anchovies (optional)   pieces of sausage, hamburger, or pepperoni

Finally, add a little salt, pepper,
1/2 Tbsp. oil, and lots of
grated cheese.

An adult should place
the sheet in the oven.

Bake at 425 - 450° for
fifteen minutes.

56

Italy

Ice cream

3 eggs
1/2 cup sugar
2 cups milk
2 tablespoons instant cocoa or coffee
1 cup fresh cream
1 teaspoon vanilla

Separate the yolks and whites of three eggs.

In a saucepan, mix:

1/2 cup sugar
one tsp. vanilla
two cups milk
two Tbsp. instant cocoa or coffee

Heat and stir over a low flame for several minutes.

The ice cream will become thicker as it heats.

Then pour it all into a dish and allow it to cool.

Next, add one cup fresh cream.

Put the dish in the freezer for at least two hours before serving.

Ham surprise

ham slices
grated Swiss cheese
cooked mushrooms
fresh cream
vegetable leftovers or
 a can of mixed vegetables

On each slice of ham, place:

grated Swiss cheese

cooked mushrooms

vegetable leftovers (pieces of cooked potatoes, carrots, etc.) or mixed vegetables from a can.

two tsp. fresh cream

Carefully roll up each slice of ham and place in an oven-proof dish.

Sprinkle Swiss cheese on top.

An adult should put the dish in an oven. Bake at 400° for fifteen minutes.

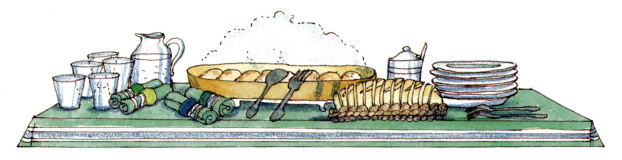

Charlotte

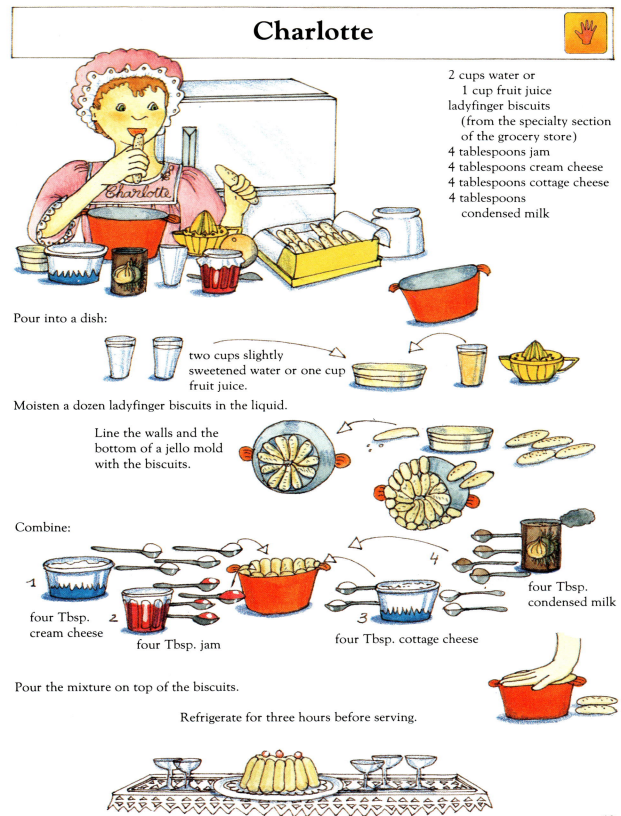

2 cups water or
  1 cup fruit juice
ladyfinger biscuits
  (from the specialty section
  of the grocery store)
4 tablespoons jam
4 tablespoons cream cheese
4 tablespoons cottage cheese
4 tablespoons
  condensed milk

Pour into a dish: two cups slightly sweetened water or one cup fruit juice.

Moisten a dozen ladyfinger biscuits in the liquid.

Line the walls and the bottom of a jello mold with the biscuits.

Combine:

1. four Tbsp. cream cheese
2. four Tbsp. jam
3. four Tbsp. cottage cheese
4. four Tbsp. condensed milk

Pour the mixture on top of the biscuits.

Refrigerate for three hours before serving.

Glossary

calcium—an element found in mainly milk products and vegetables that strengthens bones and teeth (p. 12)

calorie—a system that measures certain energy-producing values for food (p. 24)

carbohydrates—substances found in food that bring warmth, energy, and strength to the body (p. 29)

energy—power available from food to make the body and mind active (p. 8)

fats—substances found in food that give the body energy, protect against heat and cold, and cushion vital organs (p. 29)

germs—microorganisms that cause disease (p. 10)

protein—substances found in food that build and repair the body (p. 28)

vitamins—substances found in food that are essential to maintain good health (p. 26)

Index

alcohol 16
almond rice 43
apple cake 37
babies 12
banana cake 49
berries 19
bread pudding 55
breads 20
breakfast 12, 30
buffet suggestions 60, 61
caffeine 16
calcium 12
calories 24
candy 14
carbohydrates 28, 29
cavities 10, 20
Charlotte 59
cheesecake 35
chemicals 10, 14
chicken in papillotes 52
cinnamon oranges 39
coconut 20
coconut candy 33
cows' milk 16
cucumber in yogurt 42
fats 28, 29
fish, raw 46
folic acid 27
fruit salad 47
garden salad 36

germs 10
grilled ham and cheese sandwiches 54
ham surprise 58
ice cream 57
juice 16
lemon mushrooms 48
measurements 7
mocha cream 53
muesli 31
mushrooms 19
niacin 27
ounces 7
picnic 44, 45
pineapple or avocado delight 40
pint 7
pizza 56
poisonous 18
popcorn 41
pound 7
protein 28
quarts 7
rice 20
salt 14
salted cake 32
seasonings 14
steak tartare 34
sugar 20
sweet rounds 51
tabouleh salad 38
tomatoes with shrimp 50